Anonymous

The Russian Ministry of Public Education at the World's

Columbian Exposition

Anonymous

The Russian Ministry of Public Education at the World's Columbian Exposition

ISBN/EAN: 9783744726559

Printed in Europe, USA, Canada, Australia, Japan

Cover: Foto ©Suzi / pixelio.de

More available books at **www.hansebooks.com**

THE RUSSIAN

MINISTRY OF PUBLIC EDUCATION

AT THE

WORLD'S COLUMBIAN EXPOSITION.

ST. PETERSBURG.

1893.

INTRODUCTION.

CURSORY VIEW

OF

THE ORGANISATION OF THE MINISTRY OF PUBLIC INSTRUCTION.

CENTRAL ADMINISTRATION.

The chief management of the Ministry of Public Instruction established at the same time with the other Ministries, by the Ukaz of His IMPERIAL MAJESTY September 8, 1802, follows the statutes of June 18, 1863. The educational institutions dependent upon said management and extended over all the territory of the Empire, with the exception of the Grand Duchy of Finland, which has its own independent administration, are subordinated to educational district administrations (11 in European Russia, the West-Siberian district, East Siberia and the territory of Turkestan).

The chief administration of the Ministry, with the Minister and his Secretary of State at its head, consists of: 1. The Council of the Ministry; 2. Department of Public Instruction; 3. Scientific Committee; 4. Archeological Commission; 5. Editorship of the journal of the Ministry; and 6. Archives of the Ministry. The Minister of Public Instruction has moreover functionaries for special commissions.

1

1. The Council of the Minister of Public Instruction under the presidency of the Minister consists of the Secretary of State, of several members appointed by particular orders of His IMPERIAL MAJESTY; the Director of the Department, and the President of the Scientific Committee. At the Council are present also the curators of educational districts during their residence at St-Petersburg. Moreover to the Council may be invited for business concerning their jurisdiction: the President of the Archeological Commission, the permanent secretary of the Academy of Science, the rector of St-Petersburg University, and the director of the Nicholas Observatory, as well as the rectors of other universities, when they are at St-Petersburg, and others in extraordinary cases, according to the judgment of the Minister. The Council of the Minister examines: affairs and propositions requiring a new institution or considerable modifications in the different parts of the administration; cases requiring amendments to laws and institutions, explanations of such, or revocations and corrections of plans for new institutions; the annual financial estimate of the institutions of the Chief Administration, as well as of all the scientific and educational establishments under the jurisdiction of the Ministry of Public Instruction; cases of insolvency and difficulties with contracts, and deliveries and measures to avert them; complaints of private persons against the Crown, and claims of the Crown against private persons; all affairs concerning the economical measures, and exceeding the power given to the Curators of educational districts; affairs relative to the internal organisation of educational institutions and their management, such as schooling and educational matters in general, after preliminary examination of such affairs at the Scientific Committee; and finally, all affairs, in general, which the Minister deems necessary to present for examination to the Council.

2. The Department of Public Instruction, having at its head the Director and Vice-Director and consisting in addi-

tion of the secretaries, their assistants, and copyists regularly employed, is divided into several sections, each having under its jurisdiction the following subdivisions of administration: that of the inspector; that of the superior educational institutions; of ordinary male educational institutions; of primary public schools; of female schools and instructions for preparing masters and mistresses; technical and professional institutions; general affairs of scientific institutions; private and Hebrew educational institutions; pension-affairs, and the book-keeping division. The quantity of papers entering and issuing from the Department amounts to 50,000 a year.

3. The Scientific committee of the Ministry has a president, appointed by an edict of His Majesty; members nominated by the Minister of Public Instruction, and is divided into three parts:

a. The fundamental division, which examines educational questions and schemes presented by the Minister, also classic books, and programmes of teaching, books and periodical editions intended for use in educational institutions, works to be presented to personnages of the Imperial Family, schemes for expeditions, and commissions and similar scientific enterprises, plans for establishing scientific societies, reports of professors and other persons, that received scientific commissions from the Ministry and in general all affairs and questions presented by the Minister for examination of the committee. This division of the scientific committee, by request of the Minister arranges competitions for the best classic books and confers prizes.

b. A special division of the scientific committee examines elementary books intended for the lower grades as well as editions for public lectures.

c. The division of technical and professional instruction examines the affairs and scientific manuals relative to technical instruction.

4. The Archeological Commission consists of a President,

appointed by an edict of His MAJESTY, and of a certain number of members, collaborators, correspondents and artists, nominated by the President. The duties of the Commission are to edit systematically writings on the history of the country collected at the beginning of this century by an archeographic expedition and contained in the annals, chronographs, recitals and acts of the governmental judiciary. For support, the Commission receives 12,805 roubles a year.

5. The duty of the Editorship of the Journal of Ministry of Public Instruction is the publication of the monthly journal, in which all new regulations and arrangements of the Government in this respect are published, and in which the educational departments and societies are made acquainted with the course of educational progress in the Russian Empire as well as abroad. The Journal of the Ministry published by the editor and his assistants, was founded in 1802, stopped in 1829, but renewed in 1833 and issued monthly till the present time.

6. The archives of the Ministry, subject to the director, of the Department of Public Instruction, are governed by a special chief, having an assistant at his disposal. In the Archives are stored at certain terms, all documents of decisions, and of affairs of the Minister Council, Department of Public Instruction Scientific Committee, Archeological Commission and Editorship of Journal of Ministry.

LOCAL ADMINISTRATION.

In educational respects the Russian Empire is divided in twelve school districts, namely:

1. St. Petersburg district, which comprises the governments of St. Petersburg, Novgorod, Pskov, Vologda, Olonetsk and Archangel, extending over an area of 1,432,935 sq. versts (636,860 sq. miles) with 5,635,952 inhabitants.

2. Moscow district-governments: Moscow, Vladimir, Kaluga, Kostroma, Nizhni-Novgorod, Orel, Riazan, Smolensk, Tver, Tula and Yaroslav occupying an area of 461,562 sq. versts (205,138 sq. miles) with 16,685,393 inhabitants.

3. Kiev district-governments: Kiev, Podolsk, Volynsk, Poltava, Chernigov, occupying an area of 234,762 sq. versts (104,338 sq. miles) with 12,142,581 inhabitants.

4. Kasan district-governments: Kasan, Viatka, Samara, Saratov, Simbirsk and Astrakhan, extending over an area of 649,305 sq. versts (288,580 sq. miles), with 11,088,099 inhabitants.

5. Kharkov district-governments: Kharkov, Voronezh, Kursk, Pensa, Tambov, and the domains of the Don Cossaks, occupying an area of 383,887 sq. versts (170,616 sq. miles) with 13,034,550 inhabitants.

6. Vilna district-governments: Vilna, Vitebsk, Grodno, Kovno, Minsk, Mogilev occupying an area of 269,285 sq. versts (119,682 sq. miles), with 8,213,551 inhabitants.

7. Odessa district-governments: Bessarabia, Kherson, Ekaterinoslav, and Tauride, occupying an area of 214,188 sq. versts (95,194 sq. miles) with 6,100,943 inhabitants.

8. Orenburg district-governments: Perm, Orenburg, Ufa, Ural and Turgay domains, occupying an area of 1,284,741 sq. versts (570,996 sq. miles) with 6,627,746 inhabitants.

9. Warsaw district-governments: Warsaw, Kalish, Lomzha, Plotsk, Radom, Suvalki, Petrokov, Lublinsk, Sedletz and Keletz occupying an area of 111,875 sq. versts (49,722 sq. miles) with 7,960,304 inhabitants.

10. Dorpat district-governments: Livland, Kurland, Estland, occupying an area of 83,092 sq. versts (36,929 sq. miles) with 1,870,730 inhabitants.

11. Caucasus district-governments: Baku, Elisabethpol, Kutaïs, Stavropol, Tiflis, Erivan and domains: Dagestan, Kars, Kuban and Tersk, occupying an area of 408,779 sq. versts (181,679 sq. miles) with 7,261,615 inhabitants.

12. West Siberian district-governments: Tomsk, Tobolsk and domains: Akmolinsk, Semipalatinsk and Semiretchinsk, occupying an area of 3,271,078 sq. versts (1,453,813 sq. miles) with 4,217;328 inhabitants.

Moreover, to the educational districts belong the East Siberia, Turkestan and Amour domains, subject to the Governors General, who in respect to educational institutions have the same rights as the curators of educational districts of European Russia.

At the head of each educational district is a Curator, appointed by His Majesty the Emperor by representation of the Minister, of Public Instruction. The curators of the districts: St. Petersburg, Moscow, Kasan, Kiev, Vilna and Warsaw have secretaries. The curator is the highest representative of the Ministry in the district and all the educational institutions are subject to his direct jurisdiction.

Besides the general superintendence over the course of public instruction, and over the activity and conduct of the teaching personelle and students, the Curator has to fill vacancies in the district, but the appointment of directors for public and middle schools is subject to the approval of the Minister of Public Instruction. The curators make annually a detailed report upon the state and activity of the institutions that enter into the juristiction of their respective districts.

Independent of the secretaries, the curators have from one to four district inspectors at their disposal, whose duties are to inspect the course of affairs in their respective institutions.

A Curator Council exists also at every curatorship, which consists of a secretary of the Curator, district inspectors, directors of high and public schools; in districts where there is a university or some other high-class institution the rector or director of such establishment also belongs to the Curator Council. Besides this, deans of the historico-philological and math-

ematical faculties, as well as six professors of Russian language
and literature, ancient languages, history, mathematies natural history and pedagogics, and appointed by the University,
also participate in the affairs of the council on educational
questions. Affairs that enter into the jurisdiction of the
council are delinquencies of the functionaries and teaching
personelle; debatable and juridical questions with private persons, as for example, purchases and sales, construction and
rent of school-buildings, ratification of estimates on sums
exceeding 30,000 roubles, and educational affairs: the opening
and closing of educational institutions, measures of improving
instruction, examination of classic manuals, collection of systematical data concerning the course of the educational progress
and written examination of scholars terminating the course of
institutions.

The direct superintendence of the elementary public schools
is confided to the curators of the districts, but in considera-
tion of the different local conditions, it could not be organised
everywhere in the same way.

In all governments, where the zemsky regulation of Jan. 5
1864 * is introduced, the superintendence of the elementary
schools and the duty of taking measures for their develop-
ment in educational matters belong to the district and
government marshals of nobility and to the district and
governmental school-councils. The special charge of the work
of public instruction is committed to the director of public
schools appointed by the Minister of Public Instruction, and
certain inspectors. The district and governmental school councils, presided over by marshals of nobility, consist of three

members, appointed by the Ministers of Public Instruction and of the Interior, and by the local diocesan authorities respectively; of two members appointed by the district and governmental zemstvo; and finally of one member appointed by the town, if the latter participates in the maintenance of the schools. At the sessions of the council are present guardians of separate schools and the zemsky doctor, but with a special permit for each time, from the Ministry of Public Instruction. In places, where there are no district nor governmental marshals of nobility, as for example in all the districts of the Olonets government, and in several districts of the Vologda government the presidency of the school councils is entrusted to the directors and inspectors of public schools.

The district school councils have in view, the finding of means and discussion of measures to open new schools and to ameliorate the old; they also take care of providing the schools with books and other necessary accessories; they appoint masters and mistresses recommended by the inspector; they present for appointment to the governmental school councils honorable guardians of public schools; they request rewards for teachers, close such institutions as are not satisfactory; they invite teachers and finally examine the reports made annually by the inspector concerning the state of public instruction in their the respective districts.

The governmental school council has the general superintendence over the elementary schools of the government. It examines the conclusions of the director of public schools made on the reports of the district councils; divides between schools, and teachers the money subsidies from the sums sent to its disposal by the Ministry; examines complaints made on the district school councils and all affairs of discord between the members of the district school council and its President. Complaints on the judgment of the governmental school council are directed to the first department of the

Government Senate or, in case of educational questions, to the Ministry of Public instruction.

The Director of public-schools is entrusted with the direct superintendence over schools of a certain government; he is obliged to inspect them personally as often as possible, and to watch that the inspectors subject to him visit as often as possible the district confided to them.

The director is a life-member of the governmental school council, for which he annually makes reports upon the state of elementary instruction. In the district school councils the inspector replaces the director. The director as well as the inspector of the public schools ought to make a report to the Ministry after each revision of the institution. Independent of this the director of public schools has the direct superintendence over model elementary schools, established by the Ministry of Public Instruction in all governments supported by the zemstvos, country and town societies. These schools are not subordinated to the school-councils.

The elementary schools of the three governments Kiev, Podolsk and Volinsk are subject to the inspection of public schools consisting of fourteen inspectors and presided by the curator of the educational district.

In the Vilna educational district six supervisions of public schools are established, namely: in Vilna, Grodno, Kovno, Minsk, Mogilev and Vitebsk, which consist of a director, several inspectors, the number of which depends upon the number of elementary schools and representatives of the Ministries of the Interior and of Imperial Domains and of the diocesan authority. These supervisions have the same rights as the school councils.

In the Warsaw educational districts the elementary schools are subordinated to ten managements, namely: Warsaw, Lodz, Radomsk, Kelets, Kalish, Holmsk, Sedlets, Suvalki, Lomzha and Plotsk; the directors presiding over these managements are equalled in number to the directors of the public schools of the other educational districts, but have more extensive rights. For the town of Warsaw a special employment of an inspector is established which has the same rights as the chiefs of the managements.

In the Dorpat educational district the lower schools situated in towns are under the superintendence of two directors and ten inspectors of public schools. As to the village schools in places with protestant population they are subject to the supreme committee of country schools in the governments of Livland and the supreme commissions of country schools in the governments of Estland and Courland. In places, however, with orthodox population the elementary schools are supervised by a special council, that consists of an archbishop, the curator of the district and the director of the Alexander High School at Riga.

In the Siberian governments and domains the duties of directors of public-schools are performed by the directors and inspectors of classic middle schools, called progymnasiums. Besides, there are directors of public schools in the government of Irkutsk and the Zabaikal domain and inspectors of public schools in the Balagan district of the government of Irkutsk, government of Enisseisk and the domains, Akmolinsk and Semipalatinsk.

In governments of Archangel, Astrakhan, Orenburg and domains of Turkestan there are no school councils. In the government of Archangel the elementary schools are subordinated to one director and one inspector; in Astrakhan, two and in the domain Turkestan, three inspectors of public-schools.

In St-Petersburg, Moscow and Odessa there are special school councils, which are equal to the district councils.

In the Orenburg district a special inspector over Tartar, Kirguis and Bashkir public-schools is established and in the Kazan district, over' the Churash schools.

LAWS ON PENSIONS AND MILITARY SERVICE.

Persons in actual service at the Ministry of Public Instruction, after a certain number of years of service acquire the right to receive an annual pension from the Imperial Chancery. Administrative employes are subject to general rules on pensions and after thirty-five years of service receive the full amount, after twenty-five years only the half. Whereas persons serving in the educational department are entitled to special rights, and after serving twenty years receive a pension amounting to the half of their annual salary, and after serving twenty-five years, a sum equal to their full annual salary. But if the employé is forced to leave the actual service on account of protracted illness or from ruined health, then the term of the right to full pension is much shorter. For instance: in case of ruined health the employé who has served:

from 10 to 15 years receives one-third his annual salary
  » 15 » 20 »   »   two-thirds   »   »
  » 20 » 25 »   »   full salary.

In case of chronic illness after:

  5 to 10 years of service one-third annual salary
  10 » 15   »   »   two-thirds   »   »
  15 » 25   »   »   full salary.

Besides if the employé is a family man he receives over and above his pension a gratuity amounting to his yearly salary. Independent of the above-mentioned pensions persons in actual educational service, as for example, professors and teachers, after twenty-five years of service receive besides their annual salary an additional sum equal to one-fifth thereof, for every five years of further service.

The total amount paid for pensions at the Ministry of Public Instruction for 1891 was:

The law of January 1, 1874 appointing the military service duty for all classes of the population of the Empire, gives at the same time considerable rights to persons, who have received a certain education and who can produce testimonials from educational institutions specially named in the statutes concerning the military service duty. In this respect the educational institutions of all the ministries are subdivided into four classes. Persons, who have finished the whole course in the educational institutions of the first two classes can be in actual military service two years only, those who have passed the course in schools of the third class must serve three years and those who finished the fourth class of institutions have to serve four years.

Students of the institutions of the two first classes have the right, without being required to submit to the chance of drawing lots, to fulfil the military service duty as volunteers and thereby the term of service is shortened one half.

Students of educational institutions who attain the military age namely: twenty-one years are allowed by law to finish their education before being called to fulfil their military duties.

HIGHER EDUCATION

UNIVERSITIES.

The Russian universities, with the exception of those of Warsaw and Dorpat, are controlled by the statutes of August 23, 1884. Every university has a certain number of faculties: namely, historico-philological, physics and mathematics, laws, and a medical faculty (the latter not in the St-Petersburg and New Russian universities) the faculty of Eastern languages, only in St-Petersburg, and theology, only in Dorpat. There are special theological academies in St-Petersburg, Moscow, Kieff and Kazan, where orthodox theology is taught.

At the head of every university is the rector appointed for four years by the Minister of Public Instruction from the number of ordained professors; after the lapse of four years the rector can remain again for a like period in the same position by Imperial permission. At the head of every faculty is a deacon, chosen by the curator of the district from professors of the corresponding faculty, who is confirmed for four years by the Minister of Public Instruction. After this period the deacon may continue for the next four years by authority of the Minister. The higher administration is entrusted to the University Board, consisting of all the professors ordinary and extraordinary, under the presidency of the rector and his secretary. The management of the university under the presidency of the rector is composed of all the deacons of the faculties and an inspector. Besides this professors of every faculty assemble under the presidency of their deacons to discuss educational questions. A special inspector of students appointed by the Minister of Public Instruction on presentation of the curator of the district is charged with the care of the conduct of the students within the walls of the university, and as far as possible outside of them.

To the personelle of the university for the educational part belong the ordinary and extraordinary professors, private teachers, lecturers and persons of educational institutions.

In order to become a professor it is necessary to be a lecturer of three years, or a teacher in some other high educational institution, and besides this, the scientific degree of doctor of the corresponding science is required.

The confirmation of a professor depends upon the Minister who appoints to such position or the election of the candidate is left to the University-Board.

After twenty-five years of service professors who desire to be retained must be reconfirmed by the Minister; after thirty years the professor is retired, but keeps his title of professor, memer of the Faculty and of the Board, and has the right to give lectures for special remuneration decided by the Minister.

To have titles of private teachers scientific degrees are required; such positions may be held by teachers of other higher educational institutions as well as by persons who have acquired reputation by their scientific works. Such persons are inscribed by consent of the Faculty as private teachers, after receiving through the rector of the university the authority from the Curator of the District for such a title. The deacons and the rector superintend the teaching of private teachers; their remuneration is regulated by the Minister of Public Instruction and is paid to them from a special sum set apart for that purpose.

Persons, who desire to take a vacant chair of lecturer of modern languages must pass an examination before the Faculty and must be presented by the Board for the confirmation of the curator of the district.

Only young men who can show certificates of having passed the gymnasium of the Ministry of Public Instruction, which is a classic intermediate school of eight years course, are entitled to become students of the university; besides such students other persons who have certain public positions or occupations are allowed to attend university lectures and demonstrations.

Every regular or special student pays for attending the lectures and demonstrations: a. for the benefit of the university five roubles for every half year, and b. a special remuneration for the benefit of those, whose lectures they wish to attend at the rate of one rouble per week for the semester.

There are two scientific degrees given by each Faculty, except the Medical, master and doctor, and which are acquired in cursu. To the examination for the degree of master, or of doctor in the Medical Faculty, are admitted persons who after attending the lectures for eight or ten semesters in the Medical Faculty, have been examined before specially appointed examining commissions and who have obtained corresponding diplomas. Applicants for the degree of master, or in the medical Faculty that of doctor, must pass a verbal examination and must sustain a public thesis examination on some scientific subject before the Faculty. Applicants for the degree of doctor before any Faculty have no examinations to pass; they must only sustain publicly a thesis discussion.

The Warsaw University was organised in 1869 from the local General School; the university of Dorpat, although administered according to the Statutes of June 9, 1865, differs in its internal organisation from other Russian universities and ressembles more the type of German universities after which it was originally modelled.

There are Russian universities in the following towns: Moscow, St-Petersburg, Kazan, Kharkov, Kiev, Warsaw, Odessa, Dorpat and Tomsk.

1. The University of Moscow.

The university of Moscow is the oldest in Russia, founded in the reign of Elisabeth 1755 and is equipped with full faculties with the exception of that of Eastern languages. On January 1, 1891 there were 49 ordinary professors 32 extraordinary professors, 8 prosectors, 8 assistant prosectors, 4 lecturers and 95 private teachers, 3,473 regular and 309 special students.

The sum of 870,428 roubles was assigned by the Imperial Chancery for 1893 to cover the expenses of the university, and in 1890, 174,672 roubles for stipends and expenses for the assistance of students.

2. The University of St-Petersburg.

The Imperial University of St-Petersburg, founded in 1819, has full faculties with the exception of the Medical, instead of which there is under the administration of the

Ministry of War the Medical Academy. The personelle of the University consists of 49 ordinary professors, 18 extraordinary professors, 7 lecturers and ordinary instructers, of 1,781 regular and 54 special students.

For the expenses of the university for 1893 the Imperial Chancery assigned 349,109 roubles and in 1890, 78,555 were granted for stipends.

3. The University of Kharkov.

The Imperial Kharkov University, founded in 1804, possesses full faculties except that of Eastern languages. The list of the serving personelle showed on January 1, 1891, 53 ordinary professors, 19 extraordinary professors, 3 prosectors, 7 assistant prosectors, 2 lecturers, 22 instructors, 1,003 students and 39 lecture-attendants. The Imperial Chancery assigned for 1893 a sum of 371,400 roubles to cover the expenses of the University and in 1890, 32,616 roubles were given to students as stipends.

4. The University of Kazan.

The Imperial University of Kazan founded in 1804 has full faculties with the exception of that of Eastern languages. The prospectus of January 1, 1891 showed 43 ordinary professors, 21 extraordinary professors, 5 prosectors, 5 assistant prosectors, 3 lecturers, 41 private teachers, 714 students and 41 lecture-attendants. The Imperial Chancery assigned in 1893, for the expenses of the year, 373,540 roubles and in 1890, 50,675 roubles were paid as student-stipends.

5. The University of St-Vladimir.

The St-Vladimir University in Kiev, founded in 1833, possesses full faculties except that of Eastern languages. The prospectus of January 1, 1891, showed 57 ordinary and 16 extraordinary professors, 5 prosectors, 6 assistant prosectors, 2 lecturers, 24 instructors, 1,982 students and 62 lecture-attendants. For 1893 the Imperial Chancery assigned a sum of 366,572 roubles for the expenses of the university, and in 1890, 31,598 roubles were spent for student-stipends.

6. The University of Warsaw.

The Imperial Warsaw University founded in 1869 was transformed from a school of a higher type existing then in that town. It had full faculties except that of Eastern languages. The prospectus of January 1, 1891, showed 44 ordinary and 17 extraordinary professors, 3 prosectors, 3 assistant prosectors and 3 lecturers, 1,121 students and 153 lecture-attendants. For 1893 the Imperial Chancery assigned for University expense 263,148 roubles and in 1890, 53,315 roubles for student-stipends.

7. The New Russian University in Odessa.

The Imperial New Russian University was transformed from the former Lyceum of Richelieu in 1865 and has now the following faculties: historical and philological, the faculty of laws, physics and of mathematics.

On January 1, 1891, there were 26 ordinary and 10 extraordinary professors, 4 lecturers, 29 private teachers, 427 students and 14 lecture attendants. The sum assigned by the Imperial Chancery for 1893 for the university expenses was 228,759 roubles; and 31,912 roubles were paid in 1890 for student-stipends.

8. The University of Dorpat.

The Imperial University of Dorpat was at first founded by the King of Sweden, Gustav Adolph, in 1632. Suspended in 1656 on the taking of Dorpat by the army of Tsar Alexei Michailovich, it was reopened in 1690 under the name of

‹Academia Gustaviana-Carolina". In 1699 the university was removed to Pernau where it existed till 1710. The Emperor Peter the Great, wishing to continue its prosperity, issued a special Ukaz to that effect, which however was of no avail because all the professors resigned and returned to Sweden. During the reign of Paul the question arose again for establishing a university for the Baltic provinces, but the opening of the Dorpat University took place only in 1802.

The university is governed according to the Statutes of 1865, and has faculties of laws, history and philology, physics mathematics, and medicine, and a faculty of Lutheran theology.

On January 1, 1891, there were 40 ordinary and 4 extraordinary professors, eleven teachers, four lecturers, seven private teachers and docents, and 1,694 students. The sum of 233,853 roubles was assigned from the Imperial Chancery for 1893 for the expenses of the university and 26,376 roubles were paid in 1890 for student-stipends.

9. The University of Tomsk.

The Imperial University of Tomsk founded in 1888 has only one medical faculty. January 1, 1891, there were six ordinary and eleven extraordinary professors, twe prosectors, and one assistant prosector. The sum of 200,600 roubles was assigned for the university expenses of 1893. In 1890 the sum of 10,000 roubles was paid for student-stipend.

II. INSTITUTES AND LYCEUMS.

The reorganisation in 1871 of the system of intermediate education led to the considerable improvement in the instruction of ancient languages and in view of this fact the Ministry of Public Instruction was obliged to take active measures for the preparation of teachers for Latin and Greek. To further the reform in this direction the Historico-Philological Institute at St. Petersburg was founded in 1867, specially intended for the preparation of teachers for these branches, as well as for the Russian language and history. This institute provides board and lodging for the students; and as regards the course of instruction it corresponds with the Historico-Philological Faculty of the University. The students are required to present written articles on given questions and attend the special lectures of the Institute. The conditions for entering the Institute are the same as those for the University, the course being four years. A gymnasium was founded and adjoined in 1870 to this Institute and students of higher courses practice in this gymnasium in giving lectures and teaching under the supervision of professors. The prospectus of January 1, 1891, showed one teacher of religion, eight ordinary and extraordinary professors and eleven teachers. At the same time there were 73 students. For the expenses of the Institute a sum of 117,400 roubles was assigned for 1893, this amount including 29,000 roubles appointed for student-stipends.

The former Lyceum of Prince Besborodko in Niejine, Gov. Tchernigov. On account of its failure this institution was reorganised in 1875 into a Historico-Philological Institute on the same principles as those of the Institute of St. Petersburg but with the preservation of the founder's name.

January 1, 1891, the Institute was attended by one teacher of religion, ten ordinary and extraordinary professors and four teachers; there were forty-one students at that time. For the expenses of this institute a sum of 124,150 roubles was assigned for 1893, the amount including 35,400 roubles for student-stipends.

The Lazarev Institute for Eastern Languages in Moscow was founded in 1815 and consists of two divisions: one for younger students, with a similar course as in a gymnasium, and one for older students, the so-called special classes, corresponding with the Faculty of Eastern Languages of the St. Petersburg University. January 1, 1891, the personnelle of special classes

2*

was composed of five professors and five teachers, and twenty-four students; the sum of 23,700 roubles was assigned for the expenses of the Institute.

The Demidov's Lyceum for Laws in Iaroslav was reorganised in 1870 from the Demidov's school for higher sciences, which was founded in 1805. This lyceum is intended exclusively for studying laws and is organised on the same principles as the Faculty of Laws of a University. The personnelle consisted on January 1, 1891 of six professors, three docents and four private teachers. There were 191 students at that time, and the sum assigned for maintaining the institution amounted to 50,000 roubles.

The Lyceum of Tsarevich Nicolai in Moscow, founded in 1869 on private means, has board and lodging and consists of eleven classes, eight of which, the lower ones, correspond with the type of Government Gymnasiums; students of the three higher, so-called university classes, under the supervision of special tutors attend lectures at different university faculties, where they are submitted to final examination. For the lyceum expenses for the year 1893 37,328 roubles were assigned.

For the purpose of studying agronomy and forestry there is only one special higher institution belonging to the Ministry of Public Instruction, namely the *Institute of Rural Economy and Forestry* in Novaia Aleksandria, Government of Lublin, kingdom of Poland, founded in 1869. The corps of this Institute, January 1, 1891, consisted of twenty-five persons, in this number three professors, nine docents and two teachers of special subjects. There were 105 students at the same time, namely 52 in the division of Rural economy and 53 in that of Forestry; the sum of 46,770 roubles was assigned in 1893 for the institution expenses.

The St. Petersburg Practical Technological Institute. — For the purpose of communicating to students the higher technological education this institute is divided into two sub-divisions, namely: mechanics and chemistry. The number of students is limited to 500; the educational course consists of five years; students pay 50 roubles yearly for the right of following the lectures; but there are 105 Government stipends for students that have distinguished themselves by fair progress in learning and good behaviour, if they have small means, and besides this 100 free scholarships can be issued. January 1, 1891, the Institute consisted of an educational corps of seventy persons and at the same time there were 604 students. For the institute expenses for 1893 the sum of 260,000 roubles was assigned.

On the same principles as the St. Petersburg Institute there is in Kharkov another Practical Technological Institute founded in 1885. The full number of students, the duration of courses, and the annual payment for the right of learning is the same as in the St. Petersburg Institute, but the quantity of stipends is less. There are fifty Government-stipends only, and besides this fifty students can follow the lectures free of cost. The educational corps, January 1, 1891, consisted of thirteen professors, six adjunct professors, five teachers and fourteen teachers of special objects, for extra compensation. At the same time there were 427 students, of which number thirty-eight have finished their education thus forming the first class of young technical scholars graduated from the Institute. For the expenses of this institution during 1893 the sum of 206,000 roubles was assigned.

To the same type of institutions belongs the Riga Politechnical School consisting of seven divisions: Rural Economy, Technical chemistry, Surveying of land, Engineering, Mechanical Engineering, Architects and Commerce. January 1, 1891, the educational corps consisted of seventeen professors seventeen docents and twenty-two other teachers; at the same time there were 837 students. 5,365 roubles were assigned for stipends and besides this 57 persons were admitted free with all the rights of the students. The school is supported jointly by the Government and by the town of Riga.

Last the Imperial Technical School of Moscow should be

added to this list of higher special educational institutions. The educational corps of this school consists of twelve professors, three docents, nineteen teachers and twenty-nine other agents. The Government assigned 181,320 roubles for the expenses of this institution, of which 16,000 roubles are intended for student-stipends.

To study veterinary sciences there are four veterinary institutions namely, in the towns of Dorpat, Kharkov, Kazan and Warsaw. The interior organization of these institutions is about the same as the organization of University Faculties; the full course of study lasts four years.

January 1, 1891, the *Dorpat Veterinary Institute* was attended by four professors, four docents and one prosector. At the same time there were 215 students, of which 52 had stipends or attended the lectures free of cost. For the expenses of the Institute in 1893 a sum of 40,300 roubles was assigned.

The *Kharkov Veterinary Institute* was attended on Jan. 1, 1891, by three ordinary professors, four docents, one prosector and one expert blacksmith, at the same time there were 231 students. For the expenses of the Institute 51,800 roubles were assigned for 1893.

The educational corps of the *Veterinary Institute in Kazan* consisted, January 1, 1891, of five professors, eleven teachers and ten other agents; there were 91 student at the same time. For the expenses of this institution 56,400 roubles were assigned for 1893.

In the *Warsaw Institute* there were sixteen persons belonging to the educational corps and for its expenses 24,800 roubles were assigned for the year 1893.

In January, 1878, an *Archeological Institute* was founded in St Petersburg with the special purpose of preparing professional archivists. The full course of study is two years, and in order to be admitted to this institution a complete course in some higher institution must be passed first. The course of studies consists of kaleography, Russian ancient relics, chronology, genealogy, numismatics, sphragistics and ancient geography of Russia.

———— —

Besides the above-named special larger schools and institutions existing within the limits of the Empire, the Ministry of Public Instruction endeavours to give the students of higher institutions an opportunity to finish their studies abroad with special reference to such subjects that are not taught in Russia. After the introduction in 1871 of the reform of classical education in the gymnasiums, a Russian Philological Seminary was opened at the University of Leipzig in 1873, for the study of ancient languages under the guidance of the renowned professor, Ritchel, and after his death, of professor Lipsius. After preparing a sufficient number of teachers of ancient languages, the seminary at the Leipzig University was closed, and another special seminary was opened in its stead at the Berlin University for young men who have finished the course of laws in one of the Russian universities and desire to be professors of Roman Laws. Two years are required to pass the full course, each of the twelve students there in attendance receives 900 roubles a year; the whole expense of this institution does not exceed 18,000 roubles a year.

THE INTERMEDIATE INSTRUCTION.

GYMNASIUMS AND PROGYMNASIUMS FOR BOYS.

The foundation of the first public schools of intermediate education in Russia was begun in the second half of the last century but it is only in the nineteenth century that the number of these institutions began to grow perceptibly, so that at the present time every governmental town of the Empire has at least one institution of such type.

The gymnasiums and progymnasiums for boys are administered at the present time under the statute of July 30, 1871, slightly modified and amplified by later decrees petitioned for by the Minister of Public Instruction with the aim to enlarge the original statutes relative thereto. The educational course is divided into eight yearly classes. In localities where the language of the mass of the population is not Russian, admission to the first class is facilitated by the aid of preparatory classes at the expense of the Government; the duration of the course in such classes is usually limited to one year, but it can be prolonged if desired where the Russian language is universal. But in localities such preparatory classes can be opened only at the expense of local municipalities or be supported by the payments of the students themselves. The maximum normal number of students is forty in each class except the preparatory, but for the last class there is no limit.

In cases of greater number of students, the gymnasiums and progymnasiums have the right to open parallel divisions of classes, which are supported either by the educational institution itself or by a special fund at the disposition of the Minister of National Education raised by annual assignments from the sums, received in the educational institutions.

At the head of a gymnasium is a director aided by an inspector. For the immediate wants of students each class has a special tutor, elected from the teachers, and besides this in every gymnasium there are not less then two special assistants of class tutors. In the greater part of gymnasiums the students are externes, and only a few gymnasiums give board and lodging for a limited number of students. Such boarding-schools existed in fifty-three gymnasiums January 1, 1891. Besides this in some of the gymnasiums there are student-clubs partly at the expense of certain benevolent societies, and partly from the funds received from the students. Students away from home form small clubs in private appartments; such appartments are let under the eye of teachers of the gymnasiums or of persons possessing special authority for the purpose, and are under a constant supervision of educational authorities. At the present time the Ministry of National Education is occupied in increasing the number of such institutions in the building of gymnasiums and other educational institutions, so that during the last two years twenty of such boarding clubs were opened. The annual tuition varies from 200 to 258 roubles for externes and for internes from 120 to 400 roubles. Teachers are appointed from persons who have received a corresponding University education or other higher institutions of equal rank; such persons have to pass a special examination before being appointed. The teaching corps of a gymnasium forms under the presidency of the director a pedagogical board, meeting not less then once a month and settling all questions concerning the educational part of the institution such as: the admission and grading of students, fees, discipline of students, assignment of teachers, selection of text-books and educational apparatus, and selection of books for libraries. Independently of this the Pedagogical Board elects from its own membership an Economical Committee of five members including the director and the inspector for the administration of the institution.

These gymnasiums aim chiefly to prepare young men for the universities and other institutions of equal rank, and are especially thorough in Latin and Greek, Russian and Mathematics. The curriculum, according to the program confirmed by the Ministry in 1890, is as follows: Religion, two lessons weekly in all the eight classes; Russian language with the Church slavonic and Russian literature, in the first class, five lessons; in the 2^d, 3^d and 8th, four lessons, in the 4th, 5th, 6th and 7th, three lessons weekly; Latin six lessons in the 1st and 2^d and five lessons weekly in all the remaining classes. Greek four lessons in the 3^d class, five lessons in the 4th and six lessons in the remaining four elder classes. Mathematics, namely arithmetic, algebra, geometry, trygonometry and mathematical geography four lessons in the 1st, 2^d. 4th and 6th classes, and three lessons in the 3^d, 7th and 8th classes. French or German as elected by the student, French: three lessons in the 2^d, 4th, 5th, 7th and 8th classes and two lessons in the 3^d and 6th classes; German: three lessons in the 2^d, 3^d, 4th, 5th and 6th and two lessons weekly in the 7th and 8th classes; besides the above-mentioned studies, the following form part of the program as well: history, geography, physics, logic, drawing, calligraphy, singing and gymnastics.

From the year 1888 military gymnastics are introduced in all institutions belonging to the Ministry of Public Instruction, and being obligatory, have the double aim: to furnish physical training to children and at the same time to prepare them for the future military service by making them acquainted in early age with the most important exercises of that service.

The teaching of military gymnastics was at first left to military men, but simultaneously special classes were opened in St Petersburg to prepare teachers of military gymnastics, and these classes are now regularly attended by civilians and teachers in sundry institutions.

In view of the large demand for such gymnasiums, the Ministry is opening progymnasiums of four and six classes with courses similar to those of gymnasiums.

The expenses of a gymnasium are about 52,500 roubles, and those of a progymnasium about 24,000 roubles a year. January 1, 1891, there were 177 gymnasiums for boys and 60 progymnasiums under the administration of the Ministry of Public Instruction, at the same time there were 5,177 teachers, and 59,234 pupils, out of which 10,581 were boarded and lodged by the Government. In religious belief the pupils were recorded as follows:

Orthodox, Greek church .	36,929 or 62,3 per cent		
Roman catholics. . .	10,706 „ 18	„	„
Lutherans and Reformed .	5,304 „ 9	„	„

Mahometans	298 or	0,5 per cent	
Jews	4,579 „	7,7 „	„
Other religions	1,418 „	2,5 „	„

Ninety-one per cent of student of the 8ᵗʰ class have passed satisfactorily their final examinations and received diplomas.

The following data give a general idea of the progress of teaching in gymnasiums and progymnasiums: the number of students having received during the year satisfactory grades 3, 4 or 5, with the five-grade system on all the studies in general amounted to 74,2 per cent. As to the principal studies, taken separately, the number of students who received satisfactory grades is as follows:

Russian language .	81,4 per cent	
Mathematics . .	. 80,9 „	„
Latin .	. 79,4 „	„
Greek . . .	. 80,4 „	„

PROFESSIONAL SCHOOLS.

Professional Schools of the Ministry of Public Instruction are managed under the Statutes of May 15, 1872, modified July 9, 1888, and give to young men a general and technical education.

These schools consist of six classes, out of which the two latter conform to local necessities and consist of two divisions, fundamental and commercial; to the fundamental division can be added another higher class, with the object of specially preparing young men to enter the higher educational institutions. Besides this, as in gymnasiums, preparatory classes can be opened in professional schools with similar courses of study.

The administration and educational direction in professional schools are the same as in gymnasiums; boarding-schools are rare. On January 1, 1891, only six technical schools were provided with board and lodgings for students. Boys from ten to thirteen years of age are admitted to the first class. As regards tuition it varies as in gymnasiums.

The principal subjects taught in professional schools are: Religion, two lessons weekly in each class. Russian: six lessons in the 1^s, five in the 2^d, four in the 3^d and additional classes and three lessons weekly in all the remaining classes. Mathematics: four lessons in the 1st and 6th classes, three in the additional class, and five lessons in the remaining classes. German: six lessons in the two lower classes, three in the 6th, five in the additional and four in the remaining classes, the second foreign language, namely French or English and in some localities Italian or modern Greek, four lessons in the 2^d, 3^d, 4th, and three lessons in the 5th and 6th classes. Moreover geography, history, physics, natural history, drawing, tracing, calligraphy, singing and gymnastics are taught.

Commercial divisions are added to a very limited number of professional schools. In these divisions more time is devoted to the study of foreign languages and less to mathematics; drawing and tracing is not taught, but instead of eight lessons a week are given on Commercial Correspondence and Book-keeping four lessons in each class.

The expenses of professional schools average 37,347 roubles yearly each.

January 1, 1891, there were 105 professional schools with 84 parallel classes. At the same time there were 22,677 students dividet according to religions as follows:

Orthodox, Greek faith. .	13,767 or	60,7	per cent
Roman catholics.	2,729 >	12,1 >	>
Lutherans and Reformed .	3,655 »	16,1 >	>
Mahometans . . .	262 >	1,1 »	ɀ
Jews.	1,314 »	5,8 >	>
Other religions	950 >	4,2 »	>

EDUCATION OF WOMEN.

I. HIGHER COURSES.

The question of superior education for girls in Russia was raised in 1869. On the 29th of November of that year came the permission of the Ministry of Public Instruction to organize a series of public lectures on history, philology and science.

Accordingly, soon afterwards, systematical courses for girls in Literature, Russian Grammar, Mathematics, Natural Philosophy, Russian and Universal History and Cosmography were opened in St. Petersburg and Moscow. These courses had no settled plan nor were any prelimanary studies required from the pupils.

In the year 1872 permission was granted by the Minister of Public Instruction to a professor of the Moscow University Mr. Guerrier, to open a college for girls with the purpose of affording school and home with good teachers, thoroughly instructed in educational subjects. At that college particular attention was drawn to the study of universal literature and Russian history. In the meantime the necessity of increasing the means for providing Russian girls with superior education became more and more apparent. Many of them went abroad especially to Zürich in search of scientific knowledge.

Such an abnormal state of things provoked in 1876 an Imperial Ukase, which authorized the foundation of high courses for ladies on various subjects at different universities of Russia.

In virtue of this Ukase a high course for girls was established in the same year at Kazan by Professor Sorokin, in the next year, by Professor Bestoujew-Rumin and Gogotsky at St. Petersburg and Kieff on the following conditions:

1) They were to be under the immediate and constant ⏴supervision of the district school superintendents.

2) They were to be regarded as private educational institu-

tions with the obligation to be controlled every academical year by the Board of Education.

3) Scientific instruction in the girls college at St. Petersburg was to be under the direction of the Educational Council presided over by the founder of that Institution; the general management of affairs was entrusted to a Board of Trustees, consisting of twelve members both ladies and gentlemen, all of whom have to be elected by the united assembly of the Board and the Council.

A general regulation for the college was laid aside until the month of June 1879, when special rules were published for the admission of girls, according to a code of regulations formed originally by Prince Volkonsky, the Chief Superintendent of the St. Petersburg School District. According to those regulations only such girls were admitted to the college, as were in possession of a certificate. These who were not of age were obliged to secure the approval of their parents or guardians. Strict rules were given in order to lessen the number of those pupils, who failed in passing their high school examination, being thus altogether unprepared; especially the number of noncollegiate students was also limited by the provision, that their admittance could only be granted on the responsibility of the School-District Superintendent. It was not allowed to remain two years in the same class. In the course of the same year . 1879 a grant of 3,000 roubles was provided by a special order of the State Council — an equal amount was given by the St. Petersburg Municipality.

In such manner were founded colleges for girls at St. Petersburg, Moscow, Kieff and Kazan and besides this a special girls course was organized at the third Moscow Gymnasium.

The Kieff and Kazan girls Colleges had two faculties each: the historico-philological and physico-mathematical; those in St-Petersburg were supplied with a special course of elemantary mathematics. The superior courses of professor Guerrier consist only of a historical class.

The colleges at St. Petersburg and Kieff and those of Prof. Guerrier in Moscow have a four years course each, that of Kazan of two years.

The high courses for girls at the third Moscow Gymnasium have a four years course in Natural Science and three years in mathematics.

The average number of pupils in all of these colleges was about 1,500, being equally divided between the historico-philological and mathematical sections. The capital stock of the colleges was formed out of student fees and sums, collected from concerts, evening parties, and public lectures, arranged for the benefit of those colleges by charitable societies. All that mentioned above on the organization of colleges for girls in Russia proves that they were but temporary ones. The general code of regulations, as yet, considered these colleges as private schools and only in the year 1879 rules for the admission of girls were published.

In virtue of such a state of things the present organization of the high courses is but a transitory one.

Preliminary work in preparing a general regulation for the girls colleges was begun in the year 1879, but was interrupted by the resignation of Count Tolstoy from his post of Minister of Public Instruction in the year 1880.

In the year 1884 by order of His Imperial Majesty a Committee was established, presided by the under-Secretary of State Prince Volkonsky, which was to find out the best means for the organization of superior education for girls in the Empire. In this way the course of affairs went further.

The work of the mentioned above Committee is at present brought to a conclusion and the supposition of founding the girls superior education firmly is to receive in the nearest future a legislative decision. .

The principal particulars of the new code of regulations, according to the work of the Committee were following:

1) In future the foundation and existence of high courses

for ladies is to be permitted only in case if by the interests. received from the offered funds, one-third of the charges in maintaining of such a college could be borne. By such means the existence of colleges for girls was to be secured, receiving subsidy not in credit, but in fixed revenues.

2) The present collegial system of administration is to be compensated by a special director and as to the educational part and the superveillance of the student lodgings it is to be under the care of an inspectress.

3) It is supposed to reserve the students rights in obtaining a situation of a teacher; it is therefore found necessary to give to the educational part a more practical purpose, that is, to prepare teachers thoroughly instructed on educational subjects, and able to give lessons in the girls intermediate schools.

4) In order to answer the desired purpose, the colleges are to have a system of a strictly scientific instruction, adopted to the principal subjects to the historico-philological and physico-mathematical faculties. Moreover, a high course for the acquisition of foreign languages is to be organized in order to prepare thoroughly instructed teachers for the girls intermediate schools.

Such reforms are to be accomplished soon to consolidate the superior education for girls in Russia.

II. GYMNASIUMS AND PROGYMNASIUMS.

The Ministry of Public Instruction administers only one part of institutions designed for the intermediate education of girls, whereas the greater part of these institutions is administered under the Chancellery of His Imperial Majesty and under that of the Empress Marie Institute.

Gymnasiums and progymnasiums for girls under the Ministry of Public Instruction are governed by the Statutes of May 24, 1870. Each gymnasium consists of seven year classes and the studies are arranged under two heads; obligatory studies and non obligatory. The obligatory studies are Religion two lessons a week in all the classes; Russian and Literature four lessons in the first; and three in the remaining classes, Mathematic three lessons in the five lower classes and four in the two higher besides this history, geography, natural history and physics calligraphy, handiwork, embroidery, singing and gymnastics. The studies which are non obligatory are subdivided into two heads, one of these elected by the pupil is obligatory, the first head consists of the German language, French language, drawing and pedagogy and the second French, German or English elected by the student and Greek and Latin.

At the head of these educational institutions is a directrice the educational part under the Pedagogical Council or Board under the presidency of the director of the local gymnasium or professional school, or under the presidency of another representative of the Ministry of Public Instruction, the economical management is under the administration of a tutorship consisting of the president of the Pedagogical Council, the directrice and members elected by institutions supporting the gymnasium or either progymnasium of their own means or jointly with the Government, such as town or district municipalities.

The Statutes of May 24, 1870 permit the opening at the gymnasiums for girls of an additional 8th class, specially intended for those who wish to make a profession of teaching and in which the following studies are taught:

Pedagogy, Didactics, Russian including Church Slavonic, French and German, Mathematics, History and Geography. The two first subjects are obligatory and others are elective. Besides theoretical lessons, the girls of the additional class are obliged to assist in the teaching of the lower classes.

Progymnasiums have three or four classes with the courses of study corresponding to those of the gymnasium.

3

January 1, 1891, the number of institutions administered by the Ministry of Public Instruction was 342, including 143 gymnasiums, 179 progymnasiums, three higher schools for girls, five great schools in the Dorpat educational district and twelve second great schools in the same district. At the same time there were 62,529 girls and of this number 5,925 finished the course. There were 3,868,150 roubles 88 cop. assigned in 1890 for the expenses of these 342 institutions.

SPECIAL EDUCATIONAL INSTITUTIONS.

I. INSTITUTES FOR TEACHERS.

Institutes for teachers are established with the aim of preparing teachers for town schools, which are to replace gradually district schools, as these last do not correspond any more to present educational requirements. Institutes for teachers are conducted according to statutes of 31 May, 1872, they are boarding schools with three classes of one year each. Their internal management corresponds exactly to the organization of gymnasiums for boys, and teachers of these institutes avail themselves of the same rights and prerogatives as teachers of gymnasiums.

Every such institute has a town school of two classes adjoined to it, and in this school students of the higher class of the institute practise teaching. The number of pupils is limited to seventy-five of which sixty receive stipends from the Ministry of Public Instruction and the 15 remaining for pupils educated for the account of other ministries or the paying the fees for their education.

Institutes for teachers are exclusively maintained on Government expense and for every institute 30,000 roubles are assigned yearly. Young men between sixteen and nineteen years of age are admitted in these institutes, after passing an examination corresponding to the program of the 4th class of professional

schools. The curriculum of studies consists of: Religion, Russian, Mathematics, history, geography, natural history, sketch-
ing, drawing and calligraphy, pedagogy, didactic, singing and
gymnastics; besides this in some of the institutes the teaching of manual work is introduced. January 1, 1891, there were
nine institutes for teachers in the following towns: St. Petersburg, Moscow, Bielgorod, Government of Kharkov, Kazan,
Vilna, Gluchov, government of Tchernigov, Theodosia, Tauride, government Crimea, Orenburg and Tiflis. In these educational institutions were at the same time 142 teachers, and
445 pupils, of this number 29 left the institutes before com-
pleting the course and 156 were graduated. The sum of
288,994 roubles was assigned in 1890 for maintaining these
institutes.

II. INSTITUTE FOR JEWISH TEACHERS.

The former school for rabbis in Vilna was transformed in
1874 into a Jewish institute for teachers on the same general
plan as the christian institutes in Russia; it differs only by the
number of classes, four instead of three. The educational plan
is like the plans of other institutes for teachers but besides
all the objects taught there, a considerable number of weekly
lessons ten in the 1st, nine in 2d, nine in the 3d and six in the 4th
are consecrated to the study of the Hebrew and Jewish faith. To
the institute an elementary Jewish school is adjoined for prac-
tising in teaching of the pupils of the elder class. January 1, 1891,
there were eigteen teachers at the institute in Vilna and sixty-
nine pupils of whic four have left the institute before finishing
the course of studies, and height have been graduated, for the
maintaining of the institute 33,145 roubles were assigned from
taxes received from Jews to this effect.

III. SEMINARIES AND SCHOOLS FOR TEACHERS.

These educational institutions are established for the purpose of preparing teachers for elementary schools, as the need

of such teachers is more and more felt in all the parts of the Empire. These seminaries and schools consist of three classes, each with yearly courses; the subjects taught are the same as in the institutes for teachers, but in more narrow limits. There is always an elementary school of one or two classes adjoined to each seminary to furnish the practice of teaching to students of the higher class and small workshops for teaching trades. In some of these institutions, conforming to local conditions pupils are taught rudiments of rural economy and gardening. The maintaining of a seminary for teachers with the elementary school adjoined to it costs about 17,000 roubles annually, but this cost is augmented according to the number of elementary schools adjoined to the seminaries; for instance the seminary of Kazan costs 38,400 roubles, that of Irkutsk 35,000 roubles.

January 1, 1891, there were 62 seminaries for teachers with 89 elementary schools adjoined to them. Out of the 62 seminaries two are destined for preparing female teachers and five schools for teachers of local nationalities namely: the school of Simferopol for Tartars, that of Orenburg for Kirgizes, those of Kazan and Simbirsk for Tartars and Tschuvaschs and the school in Irkutsk for local pagan nationalities. At the same period the number of teachers in these seminaries amounted to 734, with 7,130 pupils, of which 800 left before the end of the year and 1,424 were duly graduated. The maintaining of all the seminaries together with the adjoined elementary schools in 1890 cost 1,243,331 roubles.

IV. SPECIAL AND TECHNICAL SCHOOLS.

1. The higher school of trade in Lodz.

This school was founded in 1869 and is conducted according to the wants of the locality, where industrial pursuits prevail. At the present moment it consists of six fundamental classes and four parallel divisions; besides this, a Sunday commercial school and a Sunday drawing-school are annexed.

For the maintainance of this instruction in 1890, 36,000 roubles were assigned. The personal staff, January 1, 1891, consisted of 20 persons with 397 students in the trade school, and 125 in the Sunday commercial school and 51 in the Sunday drawing-school. Fourteen students finished the course of education in this school in 1890.

2. The Commercial school in Odessa.

The school is founded in 1861 and is maintained exclusively by the merchants of Odessa. January 1, 1891, in all the six classes of the school there were 497 students and of this number 39 have finished the course of studies.

3. The Institute for deaf and dumb and for the blind in Warsaw.

This institute is the only one of the type under the administration of the Ministry of Public Instruction as all similar institutions of a benevolent character belong to the Empress Mary Institution. For the maintainance of this school in 1892 a sum of 43,000 roubles was assigned. The educational staff consisted of 29 persons; the number of pupils, boys and girls were 200, 162 of those being deaf and dumb, and 38 blind.

4. The Alexander professional schools in Grodno.

The formal opening of this school took place in 1890 although the house for it was bought in 1880; and as yet only a locksmith and carpenter workshops. January 1, 1891, the educational corps consisted of five persons and twenty six pupils, of which sixteen received stipends and ten were externes.

5. The Commercial and Technical school in Moscow.

This school consisted im 1890 of seven classes, attended on January 1, 1891, by 426 pupils out of which 35 have finished the course of studies.

6. The Professional school in Krasnoufimsk.

During 1890 this institution consisted of a six-class technical school and two four-class intermediate technical educational institutions, mines and rural economy; the sum of
roubles 68,000 was assigned during the year for the maintenance of the school. January 1, 1891, there were 36 teachers,
including the director, the priest and an inspector of technical classes; at the same time there were 203 pupils out of
which 115 in the classes of general education, and 88 in the
technical classes. To this school there is adjoined a rural Russian and Bashkirian school with three classes, attended by
fourteen teachers and sixty pupils.

7. Goubkin Technical School in Kungur.

This school was founded by the Actual Councillor of State
Goubkin, who offered 85,000 roubles for its establishment. At
first it consisted of six classes, at present only four. For the
maintenance of the institution in 1890 the sum of 32,000 roubles
was assigned. January 1, 1891, the corps was composed of 23
persons, including the honorable tutor, a director and a priest,
with 49 pupils, out of which 48 attended the mechanic-engi-
neering classes and one the carpenter shop. Three students
finished a complete course of studies.

8. The lower mechanic and technical school in Omsk.

This school founded in December 1882 consists of four
classes, is provided with board and lodging and has several
workshops, namely: carpentering, modelling, cast-iron foundry,
boot-maker and tailor shops. The corps, January 1, 1891,
was composed of twelve persons, including the director and
the priest. At the same time there were 67 students, of which
62 were boarders. Six students finished in 1890 the complete
course of studies.

ELEMENTARY INSTRUCTION.

1. District and town schools.

The district schools founded in 1828 and since 1865 consisting of two or three classes, do not at present fulfill the requirements, as above mentioned; these schools are therefore undergoing a gradual transformation into town schools, conformingly to the statutes of May 31, 1872. Such town-schools are opened according to the institution for teachers of the Empire which prepares the necessary educational corps.

January 1, 1877, there still were 367 district schools with 30,480 pupils and January 1, 1891 only 168 schools with 12,830 students remained; of this number 1,027 finished the complete course of learning. The educational corps consisted at the same time of 1,027 persons All the expenses for the maintenance of this sort of educational institutions amounted in 1890 to 523,000 roubles.

Town-schools are established with the purpose of giving to pupils a complete elementary education. These institutions can have from one to six classes, but the curriculum of study as well as the time for passing the course remain always the same; the course lasts six years. Each class is attended by one teacher, assisted by one or several subteachers, according to the number of pupils. The teacher is not confined to one subject, as in the intermediate educational institutions, but he teaches all the subjects included in the curriculum of the respective class, except religion, gymnastics and singing.

The curriculum of town schools includes: Religion, Russian and Slavonic languages, Arithmetic, Rudiments of Geometry, Russian, History, Geography, Natural History, Tracing, Drawing, Singing and Gymnastics. Boys from ten to thirteen years of age, after having followed without interruption the four year course of a town-school have the right to enter the first class of a gymnasium or professional school without preliminary examination.

January 1, there were only 61 town-schools; of these 5 are with four classes, 37 with three classes, 16 with two classes and 3 with one class only; they were attended by 7,171 pupils. January 1, 1891, the number of town schools grew to 407; 3 with six classes, 6 with five, 61 with four, 214 with three, 116 with two and 7 with one class. The corps of teachers amounted to 2,693 persons and there were 51,120 pupils, of which 3,199 finished the complete course of studies.

ELEMENTARY SCHOOLS.

The district municipalities, zemstvo, town and village municipalities and private persons have the right to found elementary schools by approval of the local inspector of public schools and that of the president of the district school Council; the organization of the teaching is to be arranged according to the advice of the school Council. In order to avoid all misunderstanding which may result from the absence of any restrictions, the Ministry of Public Instruction opens standard rural schools of one or two classes and maintains them by a subsidy of the locality. The curriculum of study in such schools is obligatory to those pupils of other elementary public schools who wish to profit by the privileges of the military service granted through education; thus the elementary instruction is generally levelled and approaches more and more the Ministerial program.

According to the law of June 4, 1875, in one district there can not be more than one Ministerial standard school of two classes and two of one class. These schools receive from the Ministry yearly subsidies not exceeding 1,000 roubles for a two-class school and 226 roubles for each one-class school. Besides this contributions are given to village municipalities for building houses for schools and for furniture and interior arrangements. The teacher's salary in not less than 330 roubles, the teacher of religion, curate or deacon, receives 150 roubles in two-class schools and 100 roubles in the one-class schools. The assistant teachers receive their salaries out of the special funds of the school; a trade-professional class can be adjoined to the school, the choice of trade depending wholly on the choice and sort of occupation of the local inhabitants. The children of the inhabitants of those villages, that participate in the expenses for the maintaining of the school, can attend it free; besides that if there is room other children can be received in the school, but they must pay a fee not exceeding three roubles yearly.

Such educational institutions are established either for boys or girls, but in case of necessity schools for children of both sexes can be opened. The course of study in the two-class schools continues five years and in the one-class schools, three years. In these last the following subjects are taught: Religion, Russian language, Arithmetic and Calligraphy. The course of the two-class school includes besides the above-mentioned subjects; geography, rudiments of natural history and drawing. Moreover in both these schools singing is taught; gymnastics and gardening are taught only in well provided schools.

January 1, 1891, not including the Dorpat educational district, the number of elementary schools under the administration of the Ministry of Public Instruction was 24,515, with 50,824 teachers and 1,634,458 pupils, of which 1,272,023 were boys and 362,435 were girls; 151,152 of them finished the complete course of study. The Ministry of Public Instruction spent on elementary schools in 1870 the sum of 14,436,000 roubles.

This list does not include Jewish elementary schools, the number of which, January 1, 1891, exceeded 3,000 with 49,410 pupils, 38,527 boys and 10,883 girls; musulman schools are not included either.

Lastly there exists a whole series of elementary schools, belonging to other Ministries, namely: parish church schools and the schools for reading and writing under the ecclesiastical administration.

One of the chief difficulties, that arise in the progress of elementary instruction in Russia, consists in the considerable distances between the villages belonging to the same municipality; this circumstance, especially in winter, has a very unfavorable influence on the regularity of attendance. In order to avoid this difficulty, board and lodging are being arranged in some places and entrusted to the supervision of the school teachers.

In fact there are many more obstacles against the introduction of elementary instruction in Russia than anywhere else; they consist chiefly in the great distances, in the climate, in the too heavy school expenses and lastly in the deficiency of teachers.

The state of public instruction flourishes best in the town of St. Petersburg, where the municipalities cheerfully provide means and labor for the possible introduction of elementary instruction among the people. Fifteen years ago the number of children that frequented the sixteen elementary schools of St. Petersburg amounted only to 899. In 1892 the number was 140,000 pupils in 291 schools. The estimate assigned for public instruction amounting to 613,000 roubles forms 7 per cent of the general town expenses. Moreover the town spends considerable sums for the assistance of learned societies and high courses for women.

PRIVATE EDUCATIONAL INSTITUTIONS.

The number of private educational institutions under the administration of the Ministry of Public Instruction amounted to 121 of second grade 668 of third and 412 in 1890 to 1,226, of which 20 schools were of first grade, schools were adjoined to churches of foreign religions. Of this number 129 schools are intended for boys, 285 for girls and 812 for both sexes;

January 1, 1891, there were 47,466 pupils 23,488 boys and 23,978 girls.

SCIENTIFIC INSTITUTIONS.

THE IMPERIAL ACADEMY OF SCIENCES.

The Imperial Academy of Sciences was founded in 1725 by an ukaz of the Emperor Peter the Great and was opened in the following year. Its object, as defined by the founder, is the following: 1) to assist in the diffusion of human knowledge generally; 2) to further general education in Russia; 3) to adapt the new discoveries of science to the practical needs of the country. This establishment is subdivided into three sections: physics and mathematics, Russian language and literature, and history and philology.

On the 1st of January 1891 there were in all 40 academicians (ordinary and extraordinary) and coadjutors. At this time the library of the Academy consisted of 383,860 volumes. Over and above this the following collections and museums are attached to the Academy: 1) a zoological museum; 2) a botanical museum containing over 100,000 specimens; 3) a mineralogical museum consisting of about 70,000 different specimens; 4) a botanical laboratory; 5) the Asiatic museum of the Academy of Sciences consisting of 24,245 books, manuscripts and other objects; 6) a museum of classical archeology; 7) a physiological laboratory; 8) the Russian numismatical collection of the Academy of Sciences containing 109 gold, 6,405 silver and 9,000 brass and copper ancient Russian coins and medals; 9) a museum of ethnography and anthropology, chiefly Russian; 10) a chemical laboratory and 11) a physical laboratory.

Independent of this the Imperial Academy has the supervision of the following scientific institutions: 1) the Central Physical Observatory in St-Petersburg; 2) the Magneto-meteorological Observatory in Pavlovsk; 3) the physical observatory in Tiflis, 4) the Magneto-meteorological Observatories in Ekaterinburg and Irkutsk; 5) the chemical laboratory in St-Petersburg; 6) the printing office and type-foundry of the Academy of Sciences.

II. THE NICOLAS OBSERVATORY IN PULKOVO.

Founded in 1838, the observatory aims chiefly to make astronomical observations, to make improvements in practical astronomy, to direct the activity of other Russian observatories and to prepare astronomers, geodesians and astrophysicians. The remarkable set of astronomical instruments contains a refractor worthy of attention, of 30 inches diameter lately constructed in America to order for the Russian government. The rich library of the observatory received in 1891 an addition of 175 volumes and 116 treatise. For the maintainance of the Observatory 61,000 roubles are assigned for 1893. The corps of this institution consists of 19 persons.

III. THE IMPERIAL PUBLIC LIBRARY.

The St-Petersburg Public Library was founded in 1810 and opened to the public in 1814. The Government allowed 85,382 roubles per annum for its support. Of everything that is published in Russia, one copy must be presented to the Library. January 1, 1893 the Library contained 80,593 manuscripts, authographs and deeds in various languages, 104,560 engravings and photographs, 14,085 maps and atlases, 17,877 pieces of music, 114,283 works in 1,415,982 volumes of print. This includes 260,000 works in 311,000 volumes in foreign languages: on Russia — 46,587 works in 55,423 volumes, on Palestine — 1,913 works in 2,160 volumes, on Horace (editions and commentaries) 2,095 works in 2,321 volumes, Elzevirs to the number of 2,361 works in 2,526 volumes, Aldine editions to the number of 626 works in 694 volumes, incunabula to the number of 3,672 works and lastly the «Voltaire Library» consisting of 3,318 works in 6,902 volumes.

In 1892 the following additions were made: 31,305 works in 35,101 volumes, 2,475 manuscripts and authographs, 963 engravings, 75 geographical maps, 1,104 musical pieces.

There were 108,511 readers, who applied for 142,122 works in 206,980 volumes, 41,396 numbers of journals and newspapers, and 1,247 manuscripts.

There were 2,214 visitors.

IV. THE MOSCOW PUBLIC MUSEUM OF ROUMIANTSOFF.

Founded in 1821 in St.-Petersburg by the Chancillor Prince Roumiantsoff, this museum was transfered to Moscow in 1861 and joined to the public library of that town. Later on to these two institutions the Daschkoff ethnographical museum was annexed and at the present time the museum is composed of the following divisions: 1) department of manuscripts and Slavonic old printed books, which in 1890 received forty-three new numbers; 2) library augmented in the same year by 846 volumes; 3) department of fine arts and classic antiquities, consisting of a gallery of pictures, woodcuts and a numismatical cabinet; 4) department of prehistoric Christian and Russian antiquities; 5) the Daschkoff ethnographical museum augmented in the same year by 172 donations and six department of foreign ethnography. The maintainance of the museum in 1890 cost 35,000 roubles. There were in that year 1,534 pay and 35,830 free visitors.

V. THE CAUCASIAN MUSEUM AND THE TIFLIS PUBLIC LIBRARY.

On the initiative of Count Sollogub and thanks to the assistance of Prince Vorontsoff the Caucasian Museum was founded in 1852 in Tiflis on the expense of the Imperial Russian Geographical Society. This institution was further developed by the aid of the Grand Duke Michael Nicolaevitch, when he was Governor of the Caucasus. In 1869 the museum was united to the Caucasian Public Library and received its present name. Since that time this institution has been enlarged yearly, partly at the expense of the Government and largely by subscriptions of learned men and antiquarians. Up to the present time one hundred thousand people visited the museum.

VI. THE PUBLIC LIBRARY AND MUSEUM IN VILNA.

For the maintainance of the public Library in Vilna founded in 1867 together with the museum of antiquities opened by Count Tyschkievitch in 1855, 8,256 roubles were assigned. The library received in 1890, 487 works in 972 volumes and the museum received twenty-six new articles. There were 19,776 visitors in 1890 and in the reading-room 13,573 volumes were consulted.

VII. CENTRAL ARCHIVES OF ANTIQUE DEED BOOKS IN VILNA AND KIEV.

These two depositories of archives aim to gather and make antique documents easily accessible to Government offices and private persons, until the foundation of this institution in 1852 these documents were scattered all over the western and south western provinces of Russia in courts and other district public offices.

Of this institution there are five official employes. The following fact gives an idea of the quantity of material gathered : when some Government offices wanted inquiries to be made in the archives, the staff was obliged to look through 29 deed books of different courts containing 36,098 sheets. The whole number of deeds deposited in these archives numbers over 5,000,000.

In the Kiev archives, smaller than those of Vilna, there were on the January 1, 1891: 5,885 deed books, 454,980 separate documents and about 65,000 ancient deeds.

VIII. THE VILNA COMMISSION FOR EXAMINING AND EDITING ANCIENT DEEDS.

Founded in 1862 and conducted under the Act of November 12, 1876, this Committee is organized to examine and publish such of the ancient documents, deposited in Vilna or in other towns of north-western provinces, as present a real interest in the historical sense of the word. The staff of the Committee consists of a president and four members; the maintainance of this Committee cost 9,136 roubles in 1890.

On the two hundredth anniversary of the Peter the Great's birthday, May 30, 1872 yearly premiums of the name of this great historical personality were founded; two of these premiums ammount to 2,000 roubles each and two are af 500 roubles. These premiums are delivered to the best compilers of school books for gymnasiums, professional schools, elementary schools and lastly books for the people, to this list are added later on books on technical and professional subjects. The works are presented by their authors to the Scientific Committee of the Ministry of Public Instruction in manuscripts or printed, the Committee appoints several special commissions for the critic of these works and on the basis of the verdicts of these commission the Scientific Committee adjudicates the premiums with the confirmation of the Minister of Public Instruction.

SCIENTIFIC SOCIETIES.

On January 1, 1891 there were in the Ministry of Public Instruction 59 scientific societies. Out of this number twenty have for object of their scientific labours natural history, physics or chemistry, 14 are given to history and archeology, 18 to fine arts and literature, 8 to classical philology, pedagogy and national instruction.

Here is the list of subsidies, paid in 1892 to under following societies.

1) The Imperial Society of studying Nature, in Moscow 4,857 roubles.

2) The St.-Petersburg Mineralogical Society 2,857 roubles.

3) The Imperial Russian Archeological Society 5,000 rbls.

4) The Moscow Society of History and Antiquities 5,000 roubles.

5) Society of History and antiquities of New Russia Provinces in Odessa 2,500 roubles.

6) The Fine Arts Warsaw Society 1,650 roubles.

7) The Russian Entomological Society 3,000 roubles.

Societies of students in Natural History at the universities of: 8) St-Petersburg, 9) Moscow, 10) Kazan, 11) Kharkov, 12) Odessa, 13) Kiev, 14) Dorpat 15,500 roubles.

15) The Imperial Russian Historical Society 8,000 roubles.

16) The Imperial Moscovite Archeological Society 5,000 rbls.

17) The Historical Society of the Chronologist Nestor in Kiev 800 roubles.

To this is adjoined a list of premiums founded by the scientific Society and institutions.

The staff of the Administration at the Ministry of Public Instruction.

The Minister, Secretary of State, Member of the Imperial Council, Senator, Honourable Patron, Actual Privy Councillor Count John Davidovitch Dielanoff.

The Assistant Minister, High Master of the Court, Senator, Honourable Patron Prince Michael Siergieievitch Volkonski.

The director of the Department of Public Instruction, Privy Councillor Nicolas Milievitch Anitchkoff.

President of the Scientific Committee of the Ministry of Public Instruction, Member of the Board of Ministers Privy Councillor Alexander Ivanovitch Georgievski.

The President of the Archeological Commission. Member of the Imperial Council, Ordinary Academician, Actual Privy Councillor Anathasis Theodorovitch Bijtchkoff.

The Director of the Imperial Public Library the same.

The President of the Imperial Academy of Sciences His Imperial Highness the Grand Duke Constantin Constantinovitch.

Patrons of educational districts :

St.-Petersburg. Privy Councillor Michael Nicolaevitch Kapastine.

Moscow. Privy Councillor Count Paul Alexieievitch Kapnist.

Kazan. Actual Councillor of State Nicolai Gavrilovitch Potapoff.

Orenburg. Privy Councillor John Jacovlevitch Rostovtseff.

Kharkov. Privy Councillor Nicolai Paulovitch Vorontsoff-Viliaminoff.

Odessa district. Privy Councillor Chrizanth Petrovitch Solskii.

Kiev. Privy Councillor Vladimir Vladimirovitch Viliaminoff-Zernoff.

Vilna. Privy Councillor Nicolai Alexandrovitch Siergievskii.

Warsaw. Privy Councillor Alexander Lvovitch Apuchtine.

Dorpat. Privy Councillor Nicolai Alexieievitch Lavrovskii.

Caucasus. Privy Councillor Cycil Petrovitch Jansovskii.

Western Syberia district. Privy Councillor Vasily Markovitch Florinskii.

APPENDICES.

ESTABLISHMENTS BELONGING TO OTHER MINISTRIES.

I. The Educational Institutions in the department of the Most Holy Synod.

The greatest number of schools in Russia depend on the Board of Public Instruction and next on the most Holy Synod.

The latter deals with the ecclesiastical academies, ecclesiastical seminaries, ecclesiastical schools for boys and girls, schools of missionaries and the parish church schools.

I. The Orthodox Ecclesiastical Academies are in:

St-Petersburg — students	. . . . .	256
Moscow	»	215
Kieff	»	173
Kazan	»	146
		790

II. Fifty five ecclesiastical seminaries—one in each diocese—with the number of 1000 teachers and 16,000 pupils.

III. Ecclesiastical schools — 185. Teachers — 2,000; scholars nearly 30,000.

IV. Diocesan girls' schools 50. The number of pupils amounts to 11,000.

> *Note.* Excepting the diocesan girls' schools, kept up by the means of each diocese, the department of the Orthodox religion has 12 schools for girls of ecclesiastical state, amounting nearly to 2,000 pupils in all. Those schools are patronized by Her I. M. The Empress of Russia and maintained by the Most Holy Synod.

V. One hundred and eighty schools of missionary in the eastern governments of Russia with 5,800 pupils and 90 of such schools in the Siberian districts containing 2,200 pupils.

4*

VI. In order to propagate elementary science amidst the people and to establish them in the faith and Christian morality, 21,684 parish church schools were organized, for 625,000 children both boys and girls.

Thus every year 700,000 boys and girls get their education in the schools of the Most Holy Synod.

II. The Ministry of the Imperial Court.

The Academy of Fine Arts in St-Petersburg — 426.
School for painting, drawing, sculpture and architecture in Moscow.
The Imperial Chapel of Singers in St-Petersburg.
Two Theatrical Schools (St-Petersburg and Moscow) — 290.
The Technical school at the Imperial Factory for cutting into facets.
Nine Elementary Schools maintained by the Department of Appanages.
Elementary Schools at the Factories and mines in the Altai Mountain districts.
Schools at the Imperial Stables.

III. The Ministry for Foreign Affairs.

A section for the study of Oriental languages at the Asiatic Department.

IV. The Ministry of Finance.

	n. of pupils.
The Stroganoff Central School for Technical Drawing in Moscow	865
The Peter School of St-Petersburg Merchants' Society	506
The Alexandrow Commercial School in Moscow	615
The Moscow Practical Academy for Commercial Science	433
The Trade School of the Tsessarewitch Nicholas	329
The Empress Maria Alexandrowna girls' school for handiwork	310
The St-Petersburg Central School of Baron Schtiglitz for Technical Drawing	775

INSTITUTIONS OF THE IMPERIAL RUSSIAN TECHNICAL SOCIETY.

Three special schools in St-Petersburg.
Ten evening schools for workmen.
The Ligov school for workwomen.
Four schools for young workers of both sexes.
Twelve elementary schools for children-workers.
Handiwork classes for women at the Poutilov school. Number of pupils . 2,351

Total. 6,184

V. The Educational Institutions of the War-Department.

I. Military Academies:

n. of pupils.

1) The Nicholas Academy of the Staff Office	300
with a section for the study of oriental languages	18
2) The Nicholas Academy of Engineering	93
3) The Michael Academy of Artillery	65
4) The Military Academy of Law.	85
5) The medical and surgical Academy	750

II. Military Schools.

1) The Nicholas School of Cavalry.	244
2) » » » of Engineering.	158
3) The Michael School of Artillery.	189
4) The Paul Military School (College)	411
5) The Constantin Military School (College).	407
6) The Alexandrow » » »	391
7) The Corps of Pages of H. I. M. with elementary classes. . .	216
8) The Military-Pedagogical Seminary in Moscow	120
9) Military classes for setting boundaries in Tiflis	93

III. 21 Corps of Cadets	7,896
IV. 5 Military schools (elementary)	1,112

V. Military schools for the children of the soldiers in the Guards: in Reval and at the powder-mill in Ochta (St-Petersburg)

VI. The Admiralty.

n. of pupils.

I. The Nicholas Naval Academy.	20
The Officers' Class of Miners.	20
The Class for Miners-Mechanicians	
The Officers' Artillery Class	20
The Naval Light Company for teaching.	
The divers' school.	
II. The Admiralty Technical School	80
The Naval Corps of Cadets	320

III. Special schools for sailors at Cronstadt, Nicolaev and Vladivostok.

VII. The Educational Institutions of the Home Department.

n. of pupils.

I. The Institute of Civil Engineers in St-Petersburg	300
II. The Imperial Roman-Catholic Ecclesiastical Academy.	64
III. Thirteen Roman Catholic Ecclesiastical Seminaries.	1,094

IV. The Imperial Russian Musical Society of the Home Department
1) Two Conservatories in St-Petersburg and Moscow.

2) Eighteen music-schools and different music classes in the provincial towns.

3) Seventy four music schools and colleges.

V. Assistant-surgeon schools maintained by the country states.

VIII. The Educational Institutions of the Ministry of Justice.

I. The Imperial school of Law. This school is a privileged College for the study of law. It has elementary classes. The number of pupils amounted in the year 1892 to 345.

II. The Constantin Institute for setting boundaries (surveying). This school is to afford well instructed land-surveyors for state and private purposes. It is to have but 300 pupils every year.

III. Five boundary-schools in Pskow, Penza, Koursk, Oufa, and Tiflis. They have about 300 pupils yearly.

IX. The Educational Institutions of the Ministry of Domains.

I.

SCHOOLS OF AGRICULTURE.	n. of pupils.
The Peter Academy of Rural Economy in Moscow.	924
Seven schools of Agriculture in different Governments of Russia	1,122
Thirty one elementary schools of Rural Economy.	1,150
Three horticultural schools of the Crown.	126
Six farming schools	93
Five schools for different specialties in Agriculture and Rural Economy.	156

II.

THE MINING SCHOOLS.

The Institute for the science of mining	270
The Ural Mining school	60
The «Lissichance» school for Head-Miners.	107
The Mining school of Mr S. Poliakov.	29
The Dombrov Mining School	88
Total	4,125

X. The Educational Institutions of the Ministry of Roads of Communication.

n. of pupils.

I. The Institute of Roads of Communication of the Emperor Alexander 1. That Institute is established for the special purpose of affording highly instructed engineers for railroad and port. 300

II. 28 Technical Railroad-engineering schools 1,716
III. The Conductors' school in Vishnij-Volotshok 77
IV. The school for the science of fluvial communication in Nijnii-
Novgorod. 112

Total 2,205

XI. The Department of the Empress Maria.

I.

In St.-Petersburg.	n. of pupils.
The Imperial Alexander Lyceum.	200
The Educational Society for young ladies.	407
Alexandrer school.	311
The school of St-Catharine's Order	328
The Patriotic Institute for young ladies, with a preliminary class . . .	214
Elisabeth School	193
Paul Institute.	283
Nicolas Orphan Asylum (Institute)	501
Division for Children	126
The Class for Teachers in the French Language.	19
The Nicolas girls' school.	59
The Orphan Asylum at Gatchina.	649
The Commercial School	448
The School for the deaf-mute (with Asylum).	171
Eight girls' Gymnasium	2,806
Pedagogical College (High Courses).	240
The Progymnasium at the above-named College	199
The Gymnasium in Gatchina.	105
» » » Zarskoe-Sjelo.	129
The First Marian Girls' School.	88
» Second » » »	50
Fifteen Schools of the Patriotic Society of Women.	2,626
Two schools for daughters of the soldiers of the Guard-Regiment № 1 .	50
The same of the Guard Regiment № 2	60
The Evangelical Alexander School	50
The School at the Card-Factory	42
The School for the Clerks at the Hospital of the Church of «All Distressed»	25
The School for poor girls at Pavlovsk	36
The Demidov Professional School.	152

The Educational Institutions of the Imperial Orphan-House.

The Girls' School	45
The School for Nurses	20
The School for Women-Surgeon-Assistants	8
The Marian Seminary for Teachers at Pawlowsk	42
100 Village-Schools in various districts	2,532

II.

In Moscow.

The School of St-Catharine's Order	356
The Alexander School	208
The Elisabeth School	219
The Nicolas Orphan Institute	113
Consisting of a Division for Children	268
The Nicholas girls' school	113
The Commercial School	560
5 Girls' Gymnasiums	1,608
16 Schools of the Charitable Societies of the year 1837	848
The Marian College for young ladies	285
The Alexandro-Marian School for ladies	263
The School of the Prince of Olldenburg	115
The School for Horticulture at the Russian Horticultural-Society	50
The Surgeon-Assistants' School	119
41 Village Schools in various Districts	1,702

III.

a) Institutions for young Ladies (in Governments):

In Charkow, Odessa, Kazan, Kieff, Bjelostok, Warsaw, Districts beyond the Caucasus, Tambov, Poltava, Nijni-Novgorod, Rostov at the Don, Saratov, Eastern Siberia, Kertch, Orenburg and Orel	3,171

b) Gymnasiums:

In Astrachan, Vilna, Vitebsk, Grodno, Gitomir, Kamenetz-Podolsk, Kieff, Kovno, Minsk, Mogilev, Riazan, Saratoff and Simbirsk	5,214
c) The Boarding School of the Countess Levashoff	96
The Marian girls' school at Vishni-Volotchok	56
The Marian girls' school at Tobolsk	126

The Educational Institutions of the Empress Maria Alexandrovna for the Blind.

Such Institutions are in:

St-Petersburg, Kieff, Reval, Kazan, Kostroma, Charkoff, Odessa and Voroneje . . . .

The Educational Institution of Paul Orloff for children of the poor in
    Narva   33
The Kuban Marian School for girls in Katherinodar   199
The School for Sailors' children in Nicolaeff.   135
The Gogoev School for Armenian young ladies in Nachitchevan . . .   58
The Soulimov Boarding School for young ladies of the Nobility in
    Kieff   26
The Girls' Handiwork School of Mr L. Besack in Kieff.   49
The Trade-School in Kieff.   63

                                 Total 30,712

APPENDIX II.

RECORD

OF NUMBER AND DIVISION OF STUDENTS PER FACULTIES AND GRADES

JANUARY 1, 1891.

UNIVERSITIES.	Theology.	Historico-Philological faculty.	Faculty of Law.	PHYSICO-MATHEM. Mathematics.	PHYSICO-MATHEM. Natural History.	Medicine.	Eastern languages.	Total number of students.	Total of lecture attendants.	TOTAL.
St-Petersburg	—	122	909	394	268	—	98	1781	34	1815
Moscow	—	211	1288	416	378	1180	—	3473	309	3782
Kazan	—	23	226	51	49	363	—	714	41	755
Kharkov	—	34	250	83	49	587	—	1003	39	1042
St-Wladimir	—	50	791	201	54	886	—	1982	62	2044
Novorossisk	—	38	219	89	81	—	—	427	14	441
Dorpat	260	132	140	29	145	988	—	1694	—	1694
Warsaw	—	50	350	73	60	588	—	1121	153	1274
Tomsk	—	—	—	—	—	262	—	262	7	269
	260	662	4173	1336	1084	4854	88	12457	659	13116

RECORD

OF NUMBER OF SCHOOLS AND STUDENTS FOR INTERMEDIATE AND ELEMENTARY EDUCATION UNDER THE ADMINISTRATION OF THE MINISTRY OF PUBLIC INSTRUCTION JANUARY 1, 1891.

SCHOOL-DISTRICTS.	GYMNASIUMS & PROGYMNAS.		PROFESSIONAL SCHOOLS.		GYMNASIUMS & PROGYMNAS. FOR GIRLS.		TEACHER'S SEMINARIES & SCHOOLS.		TOWN-SCHOOLS.		DISTRICT SCHOOLS.		ELEMENTARY PUBLIC-SCHOOLS.	
	Schools	Students	Schools	Students	Schools	Students	Schools	Students	Schools	Students	Schools	Students	Schools	Students
St-Petersburg	31	7856	16	2572	38	5696	6	396	45	5017	6	356	1902	100935
Moscow	36	8269	19	3571	59	10710	9	670	89	10669	48	3621	5531	367763
Kazan	11	2812	10	1931	23	4769	7	673	44	5668	15	1021	2965	235090
Orenburg	6	1467	3	528	15	3133	3	108	20	2083	4	439	1015	70829
Kharkov	27	5081	11	2850	58	10300	6	461	31	3662	39	3343	3082	219250
Odessa	26	5059	10	2042	35	6599	5	320	31	4207	10	926	2144	157753
Kiew	23	7172	7	1654	24	4109	2	138	27	2469	5	326	1903	138532
Wilno	13	4090	7	1787	3	997	5	364	16	1874	25	1475	1514	84738
Warsaw	28	8053	3	1063	19	4481	9	680	7	1232	—	—	3265	185631
Dorpat	15	3854	7	2062	23	3539	2	206	27	4023	—	—	2161	118129
Caucasus	12	3693	8	2237	16	4308	4	282	33	6268	—	—	893	56359
West-Siberia	4	802	2	240	15	2033	1	67	17	1986	12	1038	—	6040
East-Siberia	4	747	2	140	13	1564	2	126	11	1264	4	285	268	10629
District of Turkestan	1	279	—	—	1	291	1	58	9	698	—	—	40	909
Total	237	59234	105	22677	342	62529	62	4549	407	51120	168	12830	26683	1,752587